WHEN
CLOUD
BECAME A
CLOUD

For Mum
—RH

RISE × Penguin Workshop

An Imprint of Penguin Random House LLC, New York

Copyright © 2021 by Rob Hodgson. All rights reserved.
Published by Rise × Penguin Workshop, an imprint of Penguin Random House LLC, New York. PENGUIN and PENGUIN WORKSHOP are trademarks of Penguin Books Ltd. The W colophon is a registered trademark and the RISE colophon is a trademark of Penguin Random House LLC. Manufactured in China.

Visit us online at www.penguinrandomhouse.com.

The text is set in AauxProOT.
The art was created with traditional media and an iPad, then assembled in Photoshop.

Edited by Gabriella DeGennaro
Designed by Maria Elias

Library of Congress Cataloging-in-Publication Data is available upon request.

ISBN 9780593224915   10 9 8 7 6

WHEN CLOUD BECAME A CLOUD

ROB HODGSON

RISE
NEW YORK

CHAPTER 1

CLOUD

The sky is empty.

The lake is full of water.

Look! Here comes our friend, Sun.

Sun works hard all day to warm up the lake.

Some of the water droplets in the lake get so hot that they float into the sky to cool off.

Soon, the sky is full of water droplets enjoying the cool air.

They are so excited to be together
that they get closer and closer,
until . . . they make a cloud!

CHAPTER 2

WIND

Cloud is so happy to be a cloud.
She's even made a new friend named Wind.

Wind loves to blow warm air to cold places.

Wind and Sun work together every day.
They make a great team!

Sun is always warming the air,
and Wind is always blowing it
to cooler places.

When Wind blows,
Cloud gets pushed along.

Thanks to Sun and Wind,
Cloud is blown all over the world.
Which is perfect because Cloud
loves to travel.

Cloud gets blown past noisy cities and
quiet countryside,

over tall mountains and under airplanes,
getting cooler and cooler as she goes.

NOT A CLOUD
IN THE SKY

CHAPTER 3

SNOW

Brrrrrrr.

Here's Cloud!
She has traveled to a very cold place.

Cloud is so cold that some of her water droplets start to freeze.

Look! They're freezing together
into snowflakes!
The snowflakes grow
bigger and bigger.

They get so big that they become
too heavy to stay up in the sky!
That's when they fall
to the ground as snow.

Look at me!
I'm magnificent!

When they finally reach the ground,
they cover everything in a blanket
of snow.

Cloud loves watching the snowflakes
float down below.

CHAPTER 4
FOG

At night, Wind blows a gentle breeze.

Cloud is enjoying the chilly air
when she sees something
floating below.

Are those water droplets
coming from the snow?

Hello down there!

This excites her,
and she floats down to join them.

Cloud is still a cloud,
but now she's a low cloud.

CHAPTER 5

GRAYER AND GRAYER

Wind blows a strong gust
of cool air, reminding Cloud that
it's time to float back into the sky.

She's done being Fog for now.

On her way up, Cloud notices some more
water droplets looking to cool off.

This time, she invites them to join her.

Droplets from the river,
some more from the trees,

and some from the very top of the
mountain float her way.

She didn't expect so many water droplets
to jump in!

Now she's feeling very, very full.

And when she gets too full, the water droplets
squish together, getting much bigger.

Now Sun's light can't shine through,

so Cloud starts to turn gray.

And she gets grayer and grayer.

CHAPTER 6

RAIN

Cloud is feeling heavy.
She shouldn't have welcomed
so many water droplets.
She feels like she might need to . . .

Cloud says goodbye to some
of her water droplets, and
they fall to the ground.

Some make puddles,
some help plants grow,
and some fill up lakes.

Cloud is feeling much lighter now.

CHAPTER 7

THE STORM

Oh, look! More friends.

Clouds are very friendly.
Maybe a little too friendly.

Soon, it starts to get very crowded.

Cloud needs some space, so she floats
even higher to cool off.

Some of the other clouds do the same.

Soon all the clouds have the same idea.

It's a cloud party! And it's crowded!

The clouds squish together,
and so do their water droplets.

Here we go again!

They feel like they might burst . . .
and they do!

Down comes the rain!

This cloud party is starting to get a
little wild, and Cloud is heating up!
Some of her droplets get warm,
but others stay cold.

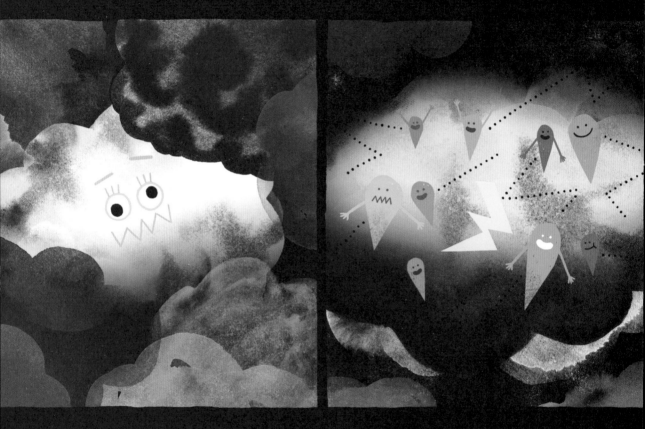

They all bump together and make
. . . an electric charge!

The charge flies out of Cloud toward the ground,
creating a bright bolt of lightning.

The lightning is so powerful that it makes a loud sound called thunder.

BOOM

It is very exciting,
and all the other clouds are impressed.

Au revoir!

Adiós!

Now that the clouds have rained out
some of their water droplets, they feel
nice and light again.
Looks like the party is over!

See ya!

Jal gayo!

As the clouds say their goodbyes,
they promise to get together
again soon.

But maybe not too soon.

CHAPTER 8
RAINBOW

After the storm, there are lots of tiny
water droplets floating in the sky.
This reminds Sun of a neat trick.

He shines his light through
the tiny water droplets, making a . . .

CHAPTER 9

THE END?

What a journey Cloud's had!
She rained, snowed, stormed,
and now she needs a good rest.

She stops when she finds a cool place
to relax over a lake.

The lake is full of water.
And here comes our friend, Sun.

Sun works hard all day
to warm up the lake.

Some of the water droplets in the lake get so hot that they float into the sky to cool off.

Soon, the sky is full of water droplets enjoying the cool air.

And when they get close together,
they join to make . . . another cloud!